Nature's
JOURNEY
APPLIQUÉ

Jane Zillmer

American Quilter's Society

P.O. Box 3290 • Paducah, KY 42002-3290
Fax 270-898-1173 • e-mail: orders@AQSquilt.com

Located in Paducah, Kentucky, the American Quilter's Society (AQS) is dedicated to promoting the accomplishments of today's quilters. Through its publications and events, AQS strives to honor today's quiltmakers and their work and to inspire future creativity and innovation in quiltmaking.

EXECUTIVE BOOK EDITOR: ELAINE BRELSFORD
BOOK EDITOR: KATHY DAVIS
COPY EDITOR: CHRYSTAL ABHALTER
GRAPHIC DESIGN: ELAINE WILSON
ILLUSTRATIONS: LYNDA SMITH
COVER DESIGN: MICHAEL BUCKINGHAM
QUILT PHOTOGRAPHY: CHARLES R. LYNCH
NATURE PHOTOGRAPHY: JANE ZILLMER

Additional copies of this book may be ordered from the American Quilter's Society, PO Box 3290, Paducah, KY 42002-3290, or online at www.AmericanQuilter.com.

Text © 2013, Author, Jane Zillmer
Artwork © 2013, American Quilter's Society

American Quilter's Society
P.O. Box 3290 • Paducah, KY 42002-3290
Fax 270-898-1173 • e-mail: orders@AQSquilt.com

Library of Congress Control Number: 2013942802

COVER: SHOW ME A SUMMER DAY IN MISSOURI, detail. Full quilt shown on page 69.

TITLE PAGE: CAMELLIA, detail. Full quilt shown on page 62.

OPPOSITE: SUMMER BUNDT CAKE WITH MINT AND BLUE-BERRIES, detail. Full quilt shown on page 51.

Acknowledgments

I would like to dedicate this book to my daughters, Carla and Katy. They are an inspiration to me with their lofty ambitions, work ethic, and youthful enthusiasm.

And thanks to all of my many quilting friends who have encouraged me along the way.

Thanks to my editor, Kathy Davis, and everyone at AQS who was involved in publishing this book.

Contents

OPPOSITE: BITTERSWEET TOO, detail. Full quilt shown
on page 21.

Introduction

ABOVE: A hand-painted wooden quilt block graces my home.

If you want a golden rule that will fit everybody, this is it: Have nothing in your house that you do not know to be useful, or believe to be beautiful.

William Morris, 1880

A thing of beauty is a joy forever. Its loveliness increases; it will never pass into nothingness.

John Keats, *Endymion,* 1818

What is more beautiful or useful than a quilt? Whether it's gracing a wall, thrown over the back of a couch, or warming you at night, a quilt always adds something to a space and to your life. And it will certainly "keep" for many years to come.

I love quilts. And I love appliqué. I love designing appliqué, cutting and stitching appliqué, admiring other artists' appliqué—all of it. Appliqué adds something unique to a quilt or project and makes you want to look twice.

When my daughters were little, I sewed many of their outfits and added appliqué to most of them. Back then, I used a dense satin stitch that looked nice on simple appliqué motifs. My first appliquéd quilts were also satin stitched.

After taking an appliqué class with Debra Wagner, I started to use some of her techniques for raw-edge machine appliqué. She taught the donut-hole fusible method and also recommended using a small, narrow, zigzag stitch with fine cotton threads chosen to closely match the appliqué motif. She also heavily starched her fabrics.

Over the years, I have adapted this method and perfected my machine-appliqué technique. I don't consider myself an expert quilter, but rather am always learning new quilting techniques and tips from other quilters—and they learn from me, as well. This is one of the wonderful things about quilters; we are always willing to share with others and teach what we know. Quilters are sort of magic people; I've never met a quilter I didn't like.

After making quilts for every bed and every wall in our home, for friends and relatives, and for donating to charity, I began to make contest quilts. I keep these show quilts flat and stacked on a guest bed where no one disturbs them, not even the cats. When guests visit, the quilts are folded temporarily and put away. I also have a beautiful armoire filled with quilts that are used and rotated.

Entering competitions motivates me to make quilts that might win an award and are not only appealing and exciting to me, but to others, as well. It is always thrilling to see my quilt hanging among all the other beautiful entries, and just too fun to hear others comment as they view my quilt. I truly enjoy sharing my work with others.

The pleasure of seeing a ribbon pinned to a quilt I've worked so hard on is an extra bonus. I learn so much from judges' comments and continue to strive to improve my work. While I make quilts for fun and for others, I always produce one that is well made and may be show worthy. This is what makes my quilting the most rewarding to me—a job well done.

In the world of quilting, there is a place for everyone from the very beginner to the entrepreneur who creates a successful business. We all share a love for the art of quilting.

I hope that you will find this book inspiring, and if you are new to appliqué, you will begin to love it as much as I do. The projects included will appeal to all levels of quilters. If you don't wish to make an entire quilt, you can use the appliqués in any number of smaller projects. See the gallery on pages 77–78 for a few examples of this.

Fabric, Tools, and Supplies

Card stock folded in half with notes about additional supplies and fabrics

Card stock unfolded with fabric samples attached

Fabric

For each of my appliquéd quilts, I use many different fabrics for piecing and appliqué. I love the "scrappy look" as it creates interest in the quilt.

Like most quilters, I have an extensive fabric stash. When I begin a quilt design, I pull out fabrics from my stash which I think I might use and pile them in front of me. This helps me form the quilt design itself sometimes.

I usually need to purchase background, border, and backing fabrics. Once I start making a quilt, I keep a small portfolio of fabric samples to take with me to quilt shows and shops. This is just a piece of card stock folded in half with swatches glued or stapled inside. I write notes about additional supplies and fabric I will need on the outside of this folder.

If I see a fabric that I like, even though it's not on my list, I buy it!—usually a minimum of a half yard. I know at some point I will use it.

I do prewash all my fabrics for the simple reason that I like the way fabric feels after it is washed. This is a personal preference. *Fabric amounts listed for the quilt projects in this book allow for shrinkage after prewashing fabric.*

As you are choosing fabrics for the quilt designs in this book, do just what I do: Start with your stash, pull out that pile of fabrics you think you'd like to use, and add as needed. Use lots of different colors, prints, and textures.

Tools and Supplies

This list includes my favorite tools and supplies. See Resources on page 78 for information on where to purchase these.

Lightweight fusible web

I keep five yards or more on hand when starting a new quilt. Always pretest fusible web with a fabric swatch to make sure it is compatible.

Sharpie® Ultra Fine Point permanent marker or mechanical pencil

Use this for tracing templates onto fusible web.

Sharp-pointed paper scissors

Use them to cut donut holes from fusible web.

Teflon® pressing sheet

Build and fuse motifs with these iron-preserving protectors.

Appliqué or open embroidery foot

You need to see what you're sewing.

Thread in shades matching appliqués

I use 40-weight rayon machine embroidery thread exclusively for my appliqué. I encourage you to try it! Thread should match the appliqué as closely as possible; go slightly darker rather than lighter if you can't match it exactly.

Bobbin thread in a neutral shade

It does not need to match the top thread. I use Superior The Bottom Line™ 60-weight polyester thread in my bobbin for appliqué.

Thread for piecing, stitching borders, and bindings

I match thread top and bobbin for piecing, borders, and binding. I use #50 100% cotton thread.

Machine needles

I use #75/11 embroidery or #70/10 sharps for appliqué, universal #80 for piecing, and universal #90 for binding.

Washable fabric marking pencil

Always test a pencil on a fabric swatch to make sure it removes completely.

¼" grid graph paper

Use this for the WOODS AND WILDFLOWERS quilt.

General sewing and rotary-cutting supplies

If this is your first quilting adventure, go to your local quilt shop and follow their advice.

Other helpful tools and supplies

* Appliqué pins
* Transparency film or clear overlay sheets
* Compass
* Plastic circle templates
* ¼" and 1" graph paper (1" grid graph paper is available in a large pad. One pad lasts many years and is very useful.)
* Mechanical pencils
* Erasers
* Ruler for drawing and designing
* Groovin' Piping Trimming Tool™ cording and piping foot (if you are adding piping)
* Walking foot for applying binding
* Lint roller
* Spray starch

Designs in Nature—
Finding Inspiration

ABOVE: SHOW ME A SUMMER DAY IN MISSOURI, detail. Full quilt on page 69.

This is not a "how to design" chapter. Rather, it's the story of how I might design a quilt; my hope is that you will someday want to design a quilt, too. Even if you are using a pattern, you might try adding elements of your own or changing something in that pattern to make it unique.

The idea of design can be scary; you might feel you need an art degree or some inherited special talent. That's simply not true. Anyone can be creative and, therefore, create a design. If you think of design as an expression of what you like, what you see, and what is dear to you, it will unfold from there.

When I design a quilt, I transform what I see in the world and how I see it into a lasting work of art. My quilts portray peace and happiness. My life may not always be peaceful and happy, but the process of making a quilt and the finished product are just that—peace and happiness.

Ideas and Inspiration

Ask yourself: What do you love? What makes you feel good? What do you love to look at? Or, if you are making a quilt as a gift, think about the recipient's likes and interests. This is where you start planning a design.

It seems I have always been attracted to nature and the outdoors. I very often find my ideas and inspiration just by being outdoors—on my daily walks or snowshoeing in the woods in winter. I'm not even really thinking about it, but I'll pick up leaves and wildflowers, notice colors, and see certain things—an idea might develop from there.

Years ago, I made a flower press to dry and preserve leaves and flowers. I sometimes use these preserved leaves and flowers as actual appliqué patterns. I also keep folders of magazine photos, sketches, and pieces of wrapping paper—things I see and like.

These folders are loosely organized by subject: appliqué, new quilt ideas, technique, color, and so on. I subscribe to a number of quilt publications and also have lots of beautiful quilt books. I use my local library to check out books on nature, drawing—almost anything. All of these are valuable in helping me pull an idea together.

Going to quilt shows and absorbing all the beautiful quilts also helps all of us think about our own designs.

Sketching and Drawing

I begin a new project with my chosen idea, theme, and appliqués, and then design my quilt from there. Electric Quilt® software is a wonderful quilting program and I may use it to plan a layout for a quilt, but I still draw all my appliqués on paper.

The actual quilt block background could be a very basic Log Cabin. BITTERSWEET TOO (page 21) is an example. This simple Log Cabin block became a "blank canvas" for my appliqué design. I also used a pieced background in BUT THERE'S A BUG IN MY BOUQUET (page 77). For this quilt, I chose a traditionally pieced quilt block called Friendship Bouquet, shown on page 12, for my background and arranged the blocks so that the insects would swirl about on the lighter fabrics.

Basic Log Cabin blocks become the canvas for appliqué.

Friendship Bouquet blocks create
a textured background.

Sketching and drawing appliqués come next.
What started as a chickadee ended as a simple
folk-art bird, which doesn't really look like a
chickadee and doesn't need to.

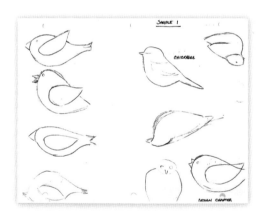

Sketches of a chickadee progress to a
folk-art bird design.

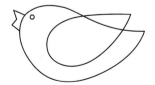

Simple folk-art bird

If I am using a pressed leaf or flower as my
appliqué, I trace the actual shape, resizing it
if needed. Sweet gum and pin oak leaves were
used just as I found them and were not resized
for SHOW ME A SUMMER DAY IN MISSOURI, page 69.

Traced leaves become appliqué templates.

Symmetrical designs are drawn in pencil on
graph paper with lots of trial and error to get
them exactly right.

Mint Cluster, a symmetrical design drawn by
author for her quilt SUMMER BUNDT CAKE WITH MINT
AND BLUEBERRIES, page 51

Once I have drawn my appliqué designs and I'm happy with them, I draw the full block design on graph paper. A large sheet of 1" grid graph paper is very helpful for this. I use pencil so everything can still be changed—and it often is! BIRDS OF HAPPINESS, a small quilt I made uses the folk-art bird shown on the right.

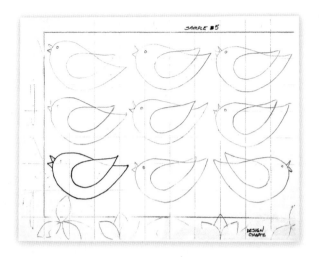

Enlargement of the folk-art bird drawing using 1" grid graph paper

BIRDS OF HAPPINESS, 9½" x 12½". Made by the author in 2012.

Prototype Blocks and Quilt Layout

If my background quilt block is a simple square, I cut one block only to start with. If I'm using a pieced block, either as a background block or anywhere in my quilt, I cut and piece one block only as a prototype.

I never cut and piece all the blocks for a quilt until I have made this prototype block. I may want to change the size or change the fabrics, and I always want to double check my pattern dimensions and the finished block size for accuracy.

Next, I fuse and cut out actual appliqué shapes from fabric (see Raw-Edge Machine-Appliqué Techniques and Tips, pages 16–19) and start laying them out on the background, using tiny appliqué pins to keep them in place.

I often change my mind about my fabric choices for appliqué, so I fuse and cut more shapes until I have the colors and fabrics just right. Any

shapes that are not used are kept in an envelope with my quilt pattern; I often use them for another project or to embellish a label. I always keep the fusible paper in place on the back of the shape until I'm ready to fuse it to the background fabric. This keeps the edges from fraying.

Often, an appliqué block or quilt layout will need to just stay pinned to my design wall and I'll look at it for days or weeks, rearranging and changing it. Sometimes, the "answer" will come to me while I'm out walking or even in the middle of the night.

Once I'm absolutely sure everything fits and I like it all, then I fuse the appliqués to the background and stitch them in place. Whenever possible, I appliqué blocks and borders before piecing them for ease of handling.

For most of my quilts, I don't plan or cut the borders until the quilt body is finished. For one thing, I'm not always sure of the finished size of the quilt. Sometimes I don't think a quilt will need borders until I see it finished, but I may change my mind and add borders after all.

I need to see the whole quilt before I can envision the borders. I love to appliqué or piece borders; I follow the same steps as when I'm planning the quilt itself—trying out appliqués or piecing designs to see what I like.

I once cut over 200 leaves for an appliquéd border design and then decided to do something totally different. Those leaves found their way into other projects, not to worry!

WOODS AND WILDFLOWERS, detail. Full quilt on page 29.

The Making of SHOW ME A SUMMER DAY IN MISSOURI

This is one of my all-time favorite quilts. The instructions for it start on page 68. I'll explain here how I created this quilt.

Each April, I visit my sister and her husband, Ellen and Larry LaVen, in Cape Girardeau, Missouri. They live about an hour and a half from Paducah, Kentucky, home of my very favorite annual quilt show, which we attend together.

One year, I also spent a week visiting Missouri in August. Summer was in full swing with very warm temperatures and lush green flora everywhere. I noticed many different leaves with such great names, started collecting them, dried and pressed them, and thought I would somehow use them in a quilt. At night, the cicadas and tree frogs were in full chorus. Everything was beautiful and memorable for this Wisconsin citizen.

Back home, I remembered saving a newspaper photo of an antique Persian rug with a mandala-like design; this photo became my inspiration for the actual quilt design. I am drawn to circles in general and use them often in my quilts.

I did not plan this quilt in any other way. I used my fabric stash and bought more fabric as needed. I simply began at the very center with a yin-yang design which signified to me harmony and balance.

Using my dried and pressed Missouri leaves as appliqué patterns, each circular row developed from there. In a swirly patchwork pattern to match the yin-yang, I pieced the backgrounds for the first two rows; the last two background rows are not pieced.

Appliquéd cicadas encircle the last row. At this point I loved the round quilt! But, it really needed a framing border, so I added the brown border. That looked too plain, so I found another leaf to add to the outside rim. Now my design looked like the sun that shone so brightly on summer days in Missouri—the Show Me State—thus the name of the quilt.

Finally, I felt the quilt needed a last framing border and chose a simple pieced-block design, but added red and green dividers for more interest. Yin-yang motifs were appliquéd to each corner block.

SHOW ME A SUMMER DAY IN MISSOURI, 89" x 89". The complete pattern for this quilt begins on page 68.

Raw-Edge Machine-Appliqué
Techniques and Tips

ABOVE: CAMELLIA, detail. Full quilt on page 62.

Over the years, I have tried different methods of machine appliqué, different stitches, threads, and a number of fusible webs and have settled on the technique I use now. It really looks good and it's fun, simple, and quick. I hope you'll try it and find it to be your favorite, too.

Strive for really nice results and your appliqué work will shine. As you are preparing and stitching appliqué using the raw-edge technique remember:

- ❀ Points should be sharp, well defined, and neat.
- ❀ Curves should be smooth.
- ❀ Starts and stops must be invisible.

❀ Motifs should be carefully fused to the background to avoid puckers and ensure that edges are securely attached.

❀ Handle motifs with care and avoid stitching into the very edge to prevent fraying.

❀ Some fabrics will still tend to fray at the edges; carefully trim stray threads with a small sharp scissors.

❀ Remove the paper backing from the fused shapes just before you are ready to fuse. If you are "auditioning" appliqués, leave the paper on as this will keep the edges from fraying.

❀ Following the pattern directions, either fuse the shapes to the background, or "build" the motifs with multiple pieces, and then fuse to the background.

Prepare Appliqué Motifs

❀ Study your project; note which appliqué templates and how many of each will be needed.

❀ Trace each appliqué template onto the paper side of fusible web.

❀ Cut out each of the shapes you have traced leaving about ¼" margin around the edges. It is sometimes helpful to label your templates by writing in the corner or edge of the paper side of fusible web.

❀ Cut out the inner portion of the fusible web, inside the traced lines, leaving about ⅛" inner margin. This is referred to as the donut hole and will leave your finished appliqués feeling soft and pliable, not stiff and "fused" feeling. I cut out a donut hole on all appliqué motifs except for the tiniest circles or leaves, or the narrowest of stems.

❀ Following the fusible web manufacturer's instructions, iron each traced shape, web-side down and paper-side up, to the wrong side of the fabric.

❀ Cut out the shapes (now fused to fabric) on the traced lines.

The templates have been traced onto fusible web, roughly cut out, and then a donut hole is cut out.

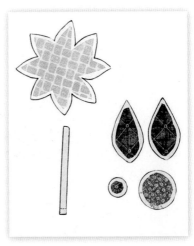

The shapes have been fused to the wrong side of the fabric and cut out on the traced lines.

Building Motifs

When multiple shapes make up one motif, you can "build" the motif before fusing it as one unit to the background. Make a copy of the motif diagram and place it underneath a Teflon pressing sheet. Prepare all the shapes you will need to build the motif and remove the paper backings. Start with the bottommost shape and lightly iron it to the Teflon sheet. Dotted lines on templates indicate that this portion will be overlapped by another shape. Iron the rest of the shapes, bottom to top, until the entire motif is complete. Be sure to let the motif cool completely, and then carefully peel it from the Teflon sheet. You can now fuse the entire motif as one unit to your background.

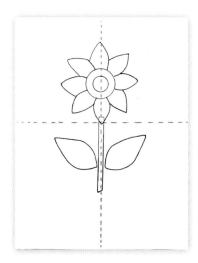

The diagram is used to build a motif. It can also be traced onto an overlay sheet for positioning the motif on the background.

Placing Motifs on a Background

Always lay out all the shapes and motifs on your background, make sure they fit, and you like the placement before fusing them in place.

Use marked horizontal and vertical placement lines, and eyeball the appliqué layout. However, you can also trace the diagrams on a clear overlay sheet and use this for positioning motifs on the background. Place a marked overlay sheet on the background and tuck the motifs in place under it. Use appliqué pins to secure the motifs as you go along.

A Note about Reversing Motifs

In general, when you fuse an appliqué motif to the wrong side of your fabric and cut it out, unless that shape is completely symmetrical, it will end up reversed on the right side of the fabric. You would need to reverse that shape before you trace it onto the fusible web.

In this book, however, ALL appliqué templates which are not symmetrical have been reversed for you. Trace them as they are printed and fuse to the wrong side of your fabric. When cut out, they will be the correct orientation.

Machine-Appliqué Stitching

This could be my favorite part of the appliqué process. I love working at my machine and I find stitching appliqué to be especially relaxing—and rewarding. If you have never done machine appliqué, I would recommend fusing a variety of simple to more detailed shapes to fabric scraps and practice stitching.

* Always pull the bobbin thread to the top when starting to appliqué stitch.
* Take three or four locking stitches; then trim the top and bottom threads.
* Using an open-toe machine-appliqué foot (foot #20 on a BERNINA), machine stitch around the appliqué motifs with a narrow, short zigzag stitch: 1.3 stitch width and 1.0 stitch length (on a BERNINA.)
* As you stitch, the needle should take one stitch on the appliqué, and one stitch off the appliqué into the background. The trick is to never let the needle hit the very edge of the appliqué as this will cause fraying. The needle should enter the background just beyond the bonded appliqué edge.
* Stitch slowly and carefully, especially around curves.
* When you reach a point, such as a leaf tip, stop the needle in the down position at the tip, take a stitch straight down, pivot your work, and then continue.
* When you end the appliqué stitching, take three or four locking stitches. Trim the top and bottom threads.

The stitched motifs show a narrow zigzag stitch using machine-embroidery thread.

Narrow zigzag stitching shows clearly in a contrasting thread and shows the point pivot.

Projects

BITTERSWEET TOO

This quilt was inspired by autumn, that "bittersweet" time of year and my favorite season. I chose rich fall colors and used a traditional Log Cabin block with an on-point setting as the base for my appliqué. The Log Cabin block has always been one of my favorites, especially since our home is a 1907 log cabin—refurbished and added onto over the years—but the original fireplace remains in use and the walls of our great room are the original log and chinking.

I machine quilted BITTERSWEET TOO on my home BERNINA machine. I chose a border feather quilting design from the book *60 Machine Quilting Patterns* by Sue Nickels and Pat Holly, Dover Publications, 1994.

BITTERSWEET TOO, 56" x 56". Designed, made, and quilted by Jane Zillmer.

BITTERSWEET TOO

Finished quilt size: 56" x 56"

Materials

Log Cabin block fabrics, cut from assorted prints, solids, and tonals

- ⅛ yard – Green
- 1 yard – Beige
- ¼ yard – Light brown
- ¾ yard – Medium brown
- ½ yard – Dark brown

Corner triangles and borders

- 1¾ yards – Dark brown

Finishing Fabrics

- ½ yard – Binding
- 3¾ yards – Backing
- 63" x 63" – Batting

Appliqué fabrics

- ½ yard – Oak leaves
- ⅓ yard – Leaves
- Circles – Scraps of light, medium, and dark brown

Fusible web and other supplies: See Resources, page 78.

Wash and press all fabrics. Spray starch fabrics for Log Cabin blocks.

Read all instructions before beginning.

Log Cabin Blocks

Finished block size: 8"

Cutting Instructions for Log Cabin Blocks

¼" seam allowance included

Before cutting all of the logs, cut and piece just one block and check your block measurement—8½" unfinished to make an 8" finished block—then cut the logs for the remaining blocks.

BLOCK A			
Log #	Color	Cut	Size
1	Green	20	1½" x 1½"
2	Beige	20	1½" x 1½"
3	Beige	20	1½" x 2½"
4	Beige	20	1½" x 2½"
5	Beige	20	1½" x 3½"
6	Light brown	20	1½" x 3½"
7	Light brown	20	1½" x 4½"
8	Beige	20	1½" x 4½"
9	Beige	20	1½" x 5½"
10	Med brown	20	1½" x 5½"
11	Med brown	20	1½" x 6½"
12	Beige	20	1½" x 6½"
13	Beige	20	1½" x 7½"
14	Dark brown	20	1½" x 7½"
15	Dark brown	20	1½" x 8½"

Block B			
Log #	Fabric	Cut	Size
1	Green	4	1½" x 1½"
2	Med brown	4	1½" x 1½"
3	Med brown	4	1½" x 2½"
4	Med brown	4	1½" x 2½"
5	Med brown	4	1½" x 3½"
6	Med brown	4	1½" x 3½"
7	Med brown	4	1½" x 4½"
8	Med brown	4	1½" x 4½"
9	Med brown	4	1½" x 5½"
10	Med brown	4	1½" x 5½"
11	Med brown	4	1½" x 6½"
12	Med brown	4	1½" x 6½"
13	Med brown	4	1½" x 7½"
14	Med brown	4	1½" x 7½"
15	Med brown	4	1½" x 8½"

Open the fabric to a single layer before cutting the corner triangles. There will be enough fabric left to cut the borders on the lengthwise grain, eliminating the need to piece them.

- Cut four squares 12½" x 12½"
- Cut each square in half twice diagonally to make 16 triangles
- Set aside the remainder of the fabric for the borders.

Log Cabin Block Piecing Instructions

I designed the Block A layout so that the darkest logs form a border when four Block As are pieced together. The lighter beige logs form the background for the center appliqués.

- The key to having the Log Cabin blocks turn out perfectly square is to pin before you stitch, stitch slowly, and press all seams open. Make sure you are using a precise ¼" seam allowance.
- Follow the piecing diagrams carefully.
- Piece 20 of Block A.

Cutting Instructions for Corner Triangles and Borders

¼" seam allowance included

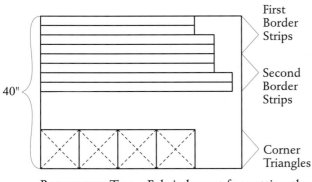

BITTERSWEET TOO—Fabric layout for cutting the corner triangles and borders

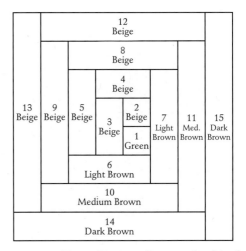

BITTERSWEET TOO—Piecing diagram for Block A

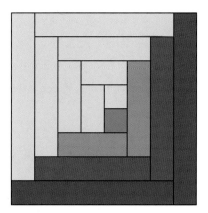

Bittersweet Too—Finished Block A – Make 20.

❀ Piece 4 of Block B.

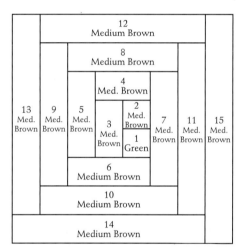

Bittersweet Too—Piecing diagram for Block B

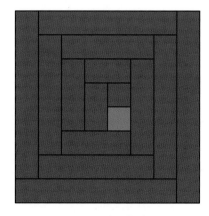

Bittersweet Too—Finished Block B – Make 4.

❀ Join the Log Cabin blocks and corner triangles to form the quilt top. Note the block arrangement in the following color diagram below.

Bittersweet Too—Full-color diagram without borders

Appliqué Instructions for the Center Motifs

Follow the general raw-edge machine-appliqué instructions on pages 16—19 to prepare all the appliqué designs.

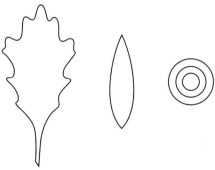

Bittersweet Too—Center Oak Leaf, Center Leaf, and Three Circles. Full-size templates are on the CD.

❋ Using the center templates, trace the motif designs onto the paper side of the fusible web. Cut out the motifs, adding an extra ¼". Cut out the inner portion of the fusible web leaving a donut hole about ⅛" inside the traced lines. Fuse the web to the wrong side of the fabric. Cut out the shapes on the outer traced lines.

❋ Remove the paper backing and fuse the center oak leaves, center leaves, and circle shapes, following the placement diagrams and quilt photo, to five light background sections.

❋ Appliqué stitch in place.

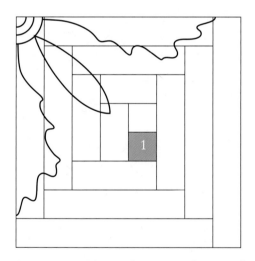

BITTERSWEET TOO—Placement diagram for the Center Oak Leaves, Center Leaf, and Circle motifs

Appliqué Instructions for the Corner Triangles

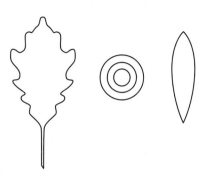

BITTERSWEET TOO—Corner Triangle Oak Leaf, Border Leaf, and three Corner Triangle Circle templates. Full-size templates are on the CD.

❋ Use the corner triangle oak leaf and circle templates to prepare the appliqués for the corner units. Fuse the corner triangle oak leaves and circles to the outer corner triangles, using the placement diagram and quilt photo for reference.

❋ Appliqué stitch in place.

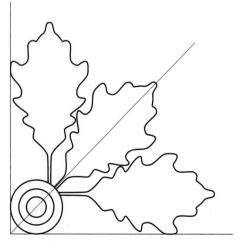

BITTERSWEET TOO—Placement diagram for the Corner Triangle Oak Leaf and Circle motifs

Cutting, Sewing, and Appliqué Instructions for Inner Border

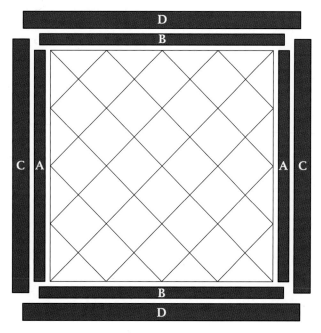

BITTERSWEET TOO—Border piecing diagram

❋ Fuse the border leaves to the A and B borders, following the diagram below for placement.

❋ Appliqué stitch in place.

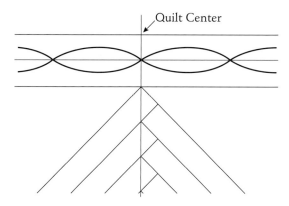

BITTERSWEET TOO—Border Leaves appliqué placement diagram

Cutting and Sewing Instructions for Outer Border

Border A

Measure the length of the quilt top along the center for the Border A measurement. Cut two border strips to this exact measurement and 2½" wide. Pin and sew one border A to each side of the quilt. Press the seams.

Border B

Measure the width of the quilt top across the center, including the A borders just added, for the Border B measurement. Cut two strips to this exact measurement and 2½" wide. Sew one Border B to the top and one Border B to the bottom of the quilt. Press the seams.

Border C

Measure the length of the quilt top along the center, including the borders added, for the Border C measurement. Cut two border strips to this exact measurement and 4" wide. Pin and sew one Border C to each side of the quilt. Press the seams.

Border D

Measure the width of the quilt top across the center, including the borders just added, for the Border D measurement. Cut two strips to this exact measurement and 4" wide. Sew one border D to the top and one border D to the bottom of the quilt. Press the seams.

BITTERSWEET TOO—Full-color diagram with borders

Finishing

Also see pages 75–76.

* Cut and piece the backing fabric to measure 64" x 64".
* Layer the quilt top, batting, and backing; baste.
* Quilt as desired.
* Stitch the binding in place and add a label and a sleeve for hanging.

WOODS AND WILDFLOWERS

L eaves, wildflowers, and thoughts gathered on my daily walks became patterns for this quilt. It is entirely appliqué; only the background blocks and borders are pieced.

WOODS AND WILDFLOWERS, 86" x 86".

Designed and made by Jane Zillmer. Longarm quilted by Lisa Arndt of Eagle River, WI.

Woods and Wildflowers

Finished quilt size: 86" x 86"

Materials

3 yards – Light background for circles

3⅝ yards – Medium brown for border frame

½ yard – Sawtooth appliquéd borders

1⅛ yards – Inner narrow appliquéd circles

3½ yards total – Scrappy log border, 8–10 prints, solids, and tonals

⅛ yard – Outer narrow border strip

8¼ yards – Backing

94" x 94" – Batting

¾ yard – Binding

Fabrics for Appliquéd Block Motifs

Use lots of different fabric scraps for the appliqués. Collect different nature-inspired shades and textures of the colors as listed for each block:

* **Wild Lupine** – Fat eighth yard of dark green and scraps of light, medium, and dark purple
* **Pinecones and Pollen** – Fat eighth yards of medium brown, gold, and dark green
* **Ferns and Fronds** – Fat eighth yard of medium green; scraps of red, light and dark green, and brown
* **Fall Aspen Leaves** – Fat eighth yard for the tree bark; scraps of light and dark brown, rust, gold, and yellow
* **Circle of Life** – Scraps of light and dark brown, medium and light green, red, black, gray, turquoise, and gold
* **Pineapple Sage** – Fat eighth yard of light green; scraps of medium and dark green, and red
* **Dusty Miller** – Fat eighth yard of light bluish-gray; scraps of gold, beige, black, dark gray, and light brown.
* **Wild Blueberries** – Scraps of blue, orange, dark brown, and medium and light green
* **Oak Leaf and Acorns** – Scraps of rust, dark and medium brown, light and medium green, and purple

Fusible Web and other supplies: See Resources, page 78.

8½" x 11" graph paper (¼" grid) – lightweight is best

Wash and press all fabrics.

Read all instructions before beginning.

Cutting Instructions

¼" seam allowance is included.

* Light background fabric for big circles:
  9 squares 20" x 20"
* Border frame fabric (surrounds circles):
  36 of Template WW

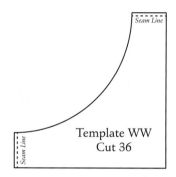

WOODS AND WILDFLOWERS—Template WW (on CD). Join at seam line.

Prepare Blocks

Make 9

Finished block: 24"

For each block:

* Sew four Template WW pieces together at the short ends (indicated "seam line" on template) to form the border frame. Press the seams open.

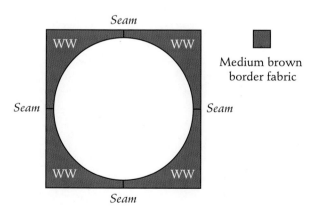

WOODS AND WILDFLOWERS—Piecing diagram for Template WW

* Turn under ¼" on the curved, inner raw edges of the pieced border frame and press.

* On the light background squares, mark the vertical and horizontal center lines with a washable fabric pencil.

* Lay the light background squares on a table right-side up; place the pieced border frame piece on the top of the background right-side up, matching the seams to the marked center lines on the light background. At each seam line, position the border frame ¼" from the raw edge of the light background.

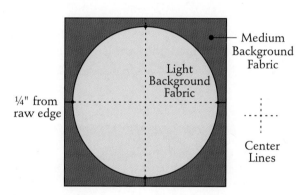

WOODS AND WILDFLOWERS—Diagram for positioning a border frame on the background

* Pin the turned-under edge of the border frame to the light background.

* Hand stitch in place. Press well.

* Turn the block to the wrong side and trim away the excess light background fabric inside the stitched circle, eliminating excess bulk and leaving a ¼" seam

allowance. See diagram 5 on page 65 in the CAMELLIA quilt project section for an example.

❀ On the right side of the light background fabric, center the Circle Template A and trace inner narrow circle/sawtooth border guideline.

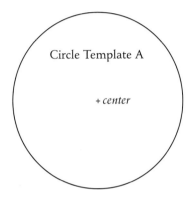

WOODS AND WILDFLOWERS—The Circle Template A (on CD) is used to mark the light background for the Sawtooth and narrow circle placements.

WOODS AND WILDFLOWERS—Light background circle with appliquéd narrow circle and Sawtooth border

Appliqué Instructions

Follow general raw-edge appliqué instructions on pages 16–19 to prepare designs.

> **Note**
>
> The Sawtooth border and narrow circle are appliquéd to the background.

❀ Prepare and cut out the Sawtooth border pieces.

❀ Prepare and cut out the narrow circles.

❀ For each block, place the outer edge of the narrow circle exactly on the Circle Template A marking. Do not fuse to the background yet.

❀ Position four Sawtooth border pieces around the outside of the narrow circle, **tucking the overlap behind the circle so just the triangles are showing.** Be sure to place the Sawtooth border pieces so that a triangle center is positioned at each background center mark.

❀ The Sawtooth border pieces do not overlap each other.

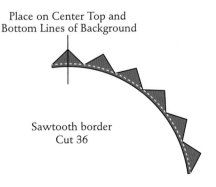

WOODS AND WILDFLOWERS—The Sawtooth border template is on the CD.

WOODS AND WILDFLOWERS—The Inner Narrow Circle template is full size on the CD.

Appliqué Designs

Notes

All templates have been reversed for you. You do not need to reverse the templates before tracing to the fusible web.

All diagrams are the same orientation as the actual quilt.

Use the diagrams to "build" the motifs before fusing to the background.

❀ It helps to do this on a padded ironing surface securing the pieces with pins placed vertically here and there as you go.

❀ When it's all in place, fuse it to the background.

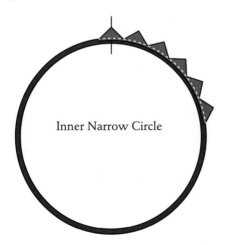

WOODS AND WILDFLOWERS—Placement diagram for the Sawtooth border

❀ Machine appliqué the circles and Sawtooth borders.

Prepare the appliqué motifs for each of the nine blocks. Lay out all the appliqués on the background using the block photo as your guide for placement. Be sure you are happy with the placement and that all the pieces fit, then fuse them to the background. Machine appliqué the motifs.

Wild Lupine Block Templates and Diagrams

WOODS AND WILDFLOWERS—Wild Lupine block

Special Instructions for Wild Lupine Stems

Use a Teflon sheet to build the appliqué motif. Cut out the stem and place it on a Teflon sheet. Next, place eight dark petals slightly behind and along each side of the stem. Be sure to leave a tiny space between each petal. To create a dimensional effect, place a light petal between each dark petal and have it peek out from between the two dark petals. Fuse. The stem is now ready to fuse to the background.

Pinecones and Pollen Block Templates and Diagrams

WOODS AND WILDFLOWERS—Pinecones and Pollen block

WOODS AND WILDFLOWERS—Wild Lupine templates are full size on the CD.

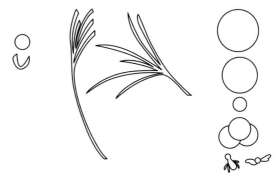

WOODS AND WILDFLOWERS—Pinecones and Pollen Block templates are full size on the CD.

WOODS AND WILDFLOWERS—Wild Lupine stem diagram. See the appliqué instructions. Make 8.

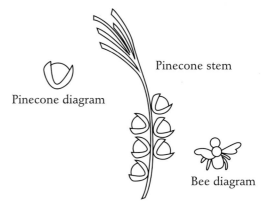

Pinecone diagram

Pinecone stem

Bee diagram

WOODS AND WILDFLOWERS— Pinecone diagram: make 56. Pinecone stem diagram: make 8. Bee diagram: make 1.

Ferns and Fronds Block Templates and Diagrams

WOODS AND WILDFLOWERS—Ferns and Fronds block

WOODS AND WILDFLOWERS—Ferns and Fronds center motif, circles, fern, and frond templates are full size on the CD.

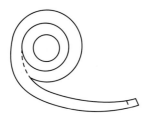

WOODS AND WILDFLOWERS—Frond diagram. Make 12.

Fall Aspen Leaves Block Templates and Diagrams

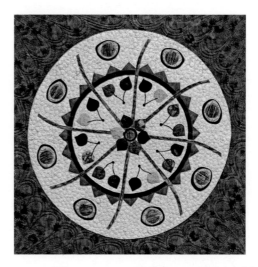

WOODS AND WILDFLOWERS—Fall Aspen Leaves block

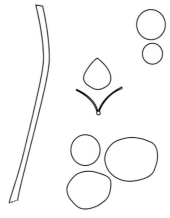

WOODS AND WILDFLOWERS—Fall Aspen Leaves branch, leaf, stem, circles, and log slices templates are full size on the CD.

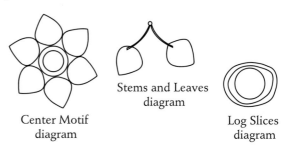

Center Motif diagram

Stems and Leaves diagram

Log Slices diagram

WOODS AND WILDFLOWERS— Center Motif diagram: make 1. Stems and Leaves diagram: make 8. Log Slices diagram: make 8.

Circle of Life Block Templates and Diagrams

WOODS AND WILDFLOWERS—Circle of Life block

Center Vine and Leaves diagram

Center Motif diagram

Outer Leaves diagram

Bird diagram

WOODS AND WILDFLOWERS— Circle of Life center vine and leaves diagram: make 4. Center motif diagram: make 1. Outer leaves diagram: make 8. Bird diagram: make 4.

WOODS AND WILDFLOWERS—Circle of Life center vine, outer leaves, center motif, and bird templates are full size on the CD.

Pineapple Sage Block Templates and Diagrams

WOODS AND WILDFLOWERS—Pineapple Sage block

Dusty Miller Block
Templates and Diagrams

WOODS AND WILDFLOWERS—Pineapple Sage center motif, Flowers, Leaves, and Stem templates are full size on the CD.

WOODS AND WILDFLOWERS—Dusty Miller block

Center Motif
diagram

Flowers and Stems
diagram

WOODS AND WILDFLOWERS—Pineapple Sage center motif diagram: make 1. Pineapple Sage flowers and stem diagram: make 8.

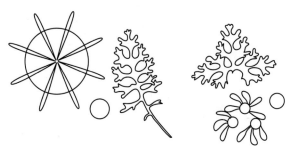

WOODS AND WILDFLOWERS—Dusty Miller center motif, Spokes, Circles and Center Leaves, Outer Leaves, Petals, and Center templates are full size on the CD.

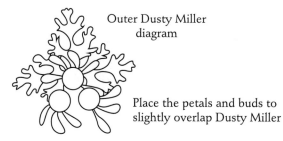

Outer Dusty Miller
diagram

Place the petals and buds to slightly overlap Dusty Miller

WOODS AND WILDFLOWERS—Outer Dusty Miller diagram. Make 8.

Wild Blueberries Block Templates and Diagrams

WOODS AND WILDFLOWERS—Wild Blueberries block

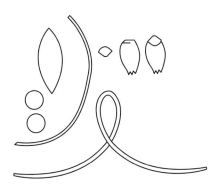

WOODS AND WILDFLOWERS—Wild Blueberries templates and Outer Vine template are full size on the CD.

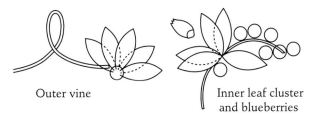

Outer vine

Inner leaf cluster and blueberries

WOODS AND WILDFLOWERS— Wild Blueberries Outer Vine diagram: make 8. Inner Leaf Cluster with Blueberries assembly diagram: make 4.

Oak Leaf and Acorns Block Templates and Diagrams

WOODS AND WILDFLOWERS—Oak Leaf and Acorns block

WOODS AND WILDFLOWERS—Oak Leaves and Acorns templates are full size on the CD.

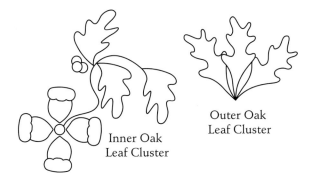

Inner Oak Leaf Cluster

Outer Oak Leaf Cluster

WOODS AND WILDFLOWERS—Inner Oak Leaf Cluster diagram: make 4. Outer Oak Leaf Cluster diagram: make 8.

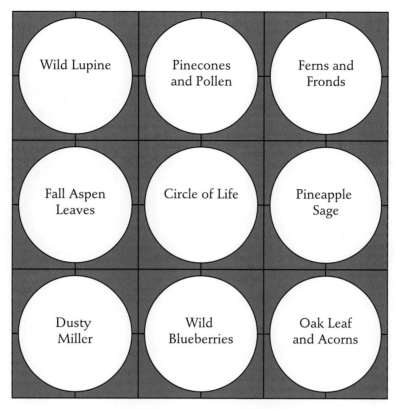

Wild Lupine	Pinecones and Pollen	Ferns and Fronds
Fall Aspen Leaves	Circle of Life	Pineapple Sage
Dusty Miller	Wild Blueberries	Oak Leaf and Acorns

WOODS AND WILDFLOWERS—Block placement diagram

Piece the blocks following the block placement diagram shown above.

Scrappy Border Piecing and Cutting Instructions

Cut about 325 logs in a variety of widths between 1" and 2" by 9" in length. This includes ¼" seam allowance. I like to cut a 9" wide strip of fabric, then cut this strip into different widths.

When stitching log-pieced borders like this one, your finished piece tends to be distorted. I devised this method to ensure perfectly straight borders.

WOODS AND WILDFLOWERS—My inspiration for pieced log borders

❀ Lay a sheet of graph paper horizontally on your work table.

❀ Place two logs right sides together with the raw edges along a graph line, near the left edge of paper. The top and bottom edges will extend beyond the page and will be trimmed later.

❀ Pin. Stitch a ¼" seam. Press the top log to the right.

❀ Place a new log wrong-side up on top of last log, raw edges even, along the graph line. Pin, stitch, and press open.

WOODS AND WILDFLOWERS—Scrappy border—one edge is trimmed, one is not.

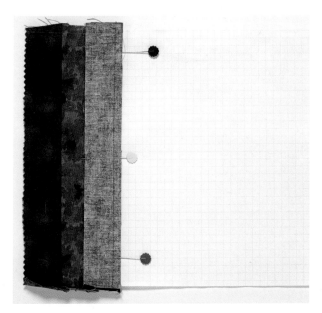

WOODS AND WILDFLOWERS—Scrappy border assembly

❀ Continue in this manner until the sheet is filled.

❀ Trim both long edges even with the paper. The borders will finish to 8".

❀ You will need to make about 33 "pages" or units. You can always add or subtract logs, depending on the widths you have cut them.

❀ Remove the paper from the back.

Log Border Units

❀ Measure the width of the quilt top across the center for the Border A measurement. Piece two log borders to this measurement. Stitch one log Border A to the top and one to the bottom of the quilt. Press the seams toward the quilt.

❀ Measure the length of the quilt top across the center, including the log borders just added, for the Border B measurement.

Piece two log borders to this measurement. Stitch one log Border B to each side of the quilt. Press the seams toward the quilt.

Narrow Inner Border

❃ I added the dark brown border to visually offset the quilt top and log border. Use the raw-edge appliqué technique and prepare ¼" strips to equal approximately 350" total.

❃ Fuse to the quilt top along the log border seam line, turning under a scant ¼" to join the strips. Appliqué stitch in place.

Finishing

Also see pages 75–76.

❃ Cut and piece the backing fabric to measure 94" x 94".

❃ Layer the quilt top, batting, and backing; baste.

❃ Quilt as desired.

❃ Stitch the binding in place, and add a label and a sleeve for hanging.

I Love the Nightlife

Insects are beautiful. Now, I don't want them in my house or sitting on my lap, but just look at this lovely Common Katydid. I found it on my sister's porch in Missouri perfectly preserved, and it inspired the insect designs in this quilt.

There are nine different dragonflies and beetles in this quilt and they replace flowers in a traditional appliqué design layout. The insects appear to be hovering about the flowers, and, on the black background, seem to be out having fun at night when we can't see them.

I LOVE THE NIGHTLIFE, 57" x 57".
Designed and made by Jane Zillmer. Longarm quilted by Lisa Arndt.

I LOVE THE NIGHTLIFE

Finished quilt size: 57" x 57"

Materials

Insects and Border Petals

1 fat eighth – Gold and white stripe for the bodies and tails

⅝ yard total – 4 to 6 different gold print scraps

¼ yard total – 3 different light brown prints

1 fat quarter – Red for flowers

Scrap – Black for flower center circles

Scraps of each – Small green and white flowers

1 fat quarter – Larger green leaves

½ yard – Swags and corner motif

4 yards – Background and borders

4 yards – Backing

65" x 65" – Batting

½ yard – Binding

Fusible web and other supplies: See Resources, page 78.

Wash and press all fabrics.

Read all instructions before beginning.

Cutting Instructions

¼" seam allowance included

Finished block size: 15"

* Background blocks
   9 squares 15½" x 15½"
* Border A (cut on lengthwise grain)
   2 strips 6½" x 45½"
* Border B (cut on lengthwise grain)
   2 strips 6½" x 57½"

Follow the general raw-edge appliqué instructions on pages 17—19 to prepare all appliqué designs.

Appliqué Instructions for Background Blocks

Flowers and Leaves

* Mark horizontal and vertical center lines on each block using a washable fabric pencil.

* Prepare and fuse a red flower with a black center circle, four green and white flowers, and four larger green leaves to each of the nine background blocks. Prepare the remaining four red flowers and set aside.

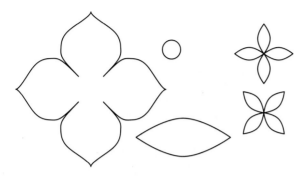

I LOVE THE NIGHTLIFE—Templates for the Leaves and Flowers are full size on the CD.

I LOVE THE NIGHTLIFE—Flowers assembly diagram. Make 36 units.

❀ Using the templates, trace the motif designs onto the paper side of the fusible web. Cut out the motifs, adding an extra ¼". Cut out the inner portion of the fusible web, leaving a donut hole about ⅛" inside the traced lines. Fuse the web to the wrong side of the fabric. Cut out the shapes on the outer traced lines.

I LOVE THE NIGHTLIFE—Diagram for the Flower and Leaf motifs placement

❀ Remove the paper backing and fuse the flowers and leaves to the nine background squares. Follow the quilt photo on page 43 and subsequent placement diagrams.

Insect Appliqués

❀ There are nine different insect designs and you will prepare and fuse four of each per block. The nose of each insect is positioned just at the tip of a green and white flower and should be placed on a center line.

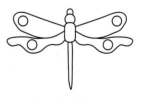

Finished diagram

I LOVE THE NIGHTLIFE—Template for Dragonfly #1 is full size on the CD. Assembly diagram: make 4.

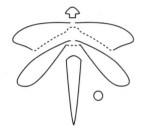 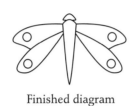

Finished diagram

I Love the Nightlife—Template for Dragonfly #2 is full size on the CD. Assembly diagram: make 4.

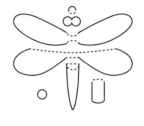 

Finished diagram

I Love the Nightlife—Template for Dragonfly #4 is full size on the CD. Assembly diagram: make 4.

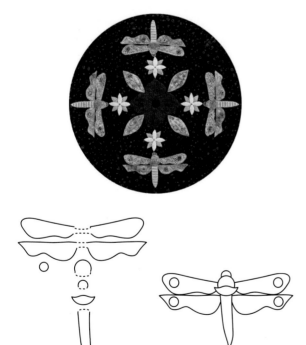

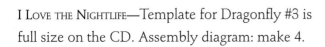

Finished diagram

I Love the Nightlife—Template for Dragonfly #3 is full size on the CD. Assembly diagram: make 4.

Finished diagram

I Love the Nightlife—Template for Dragonfly #5 is full size on the CD. Assembly diagram: make 4.

Finished diagram

I LOVE THE NIGHTLIFE—Template for Beetle #1 is full size on the CD. Assembly diagram: make 4.

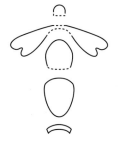

Finished diagram

I LOVE THE NIGHTLIFE—Template for Beetle #3 is full size on the CD. Assembly diagram: make 4.

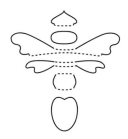

Finished diagram

I LOVE THE NIGHTLIFE—Template for Beetle #2 is full size on the CD. Assembly diagram: make 4.

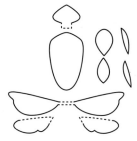

Finished diagram

I LOVE THE NIGHTLIFE—Template for Beetle #4 is full size on the CD. Assembly diagram: make 4.

❋ Following the general raw-edge appliqué instructions on pages 16–19, appliqué stitch the dragonfly and beetle motifs in place.

❋ Lay out the appliquéd background blocks in three rows of three each, alternating the dragonflies and beetles. Join the blocks and rows to form the quilt top. Press the seams open.

❋ Position the four remaining red flowers over the intersections of the center background blocks and fuse to the quilt top. Refer to the placement diagram.

Dragonfly Block #5	Beetle Block #3	Dragonfly Block #1
Beetle Block #4	Dragonfly Block #2	Beetle Block #1
Dragonfly Block #3	Beetle Block #2	Dragonfly Block #4

Red Flower Placement ✶

I LOVE THE NIGHTLIFE—Placement diagram for Dragonfly blocks, Beetle blocks, and four Red Flowers

Borders

❋ Pin and sew one Border A to each side of the quilt. Press the seams.

❋ Pin and sew one Border B to the top of the quilt and one Border B to the bottom of the quilt. Press the seams.

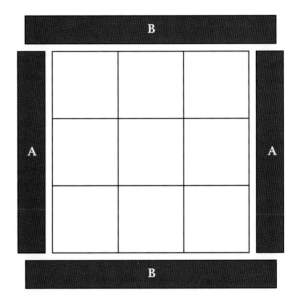

I LOVE THE NIGHTLIFE—Border placement diagram

Appliqué Borders

❋ Make a full border-swag template.

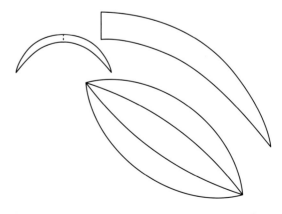

I LOVE THE NIGHTLIFE—Full Border-Swag templates are full size on the CD.

❀ Prepare the swags, border wing motifs, and corner motifs.

Border Wings diagram

I LOVE THE NIGHTLIFE—Border Wing template is full size on the CD. Border Wing diagram: make 12 units.

❀ Fuse swags and motifs to the borders and background following the swags and motifs border placement diagram.

I LOVE THE NIGHTLIFE—Swags and Motifs Border placement diagram is full size on the CD.

❀ Appliqué stitch in place.

Finishing
Also see pages 75–76.

❀ Cut and piece the backing fabric to measure 65" x 65".

❀ Layer the quilt top, batting, and backing; baste.

❀ Quilt as desired.

❀ Stitch the binding in place, and add a label and a sleeve for hanging.

SUMMER BUNDT CAKE WITH MINT AND BLUEBERRIES

This quilt was inspired by my sister Ellen's original recipe by the same name. I tried the recipe and when I looked at the top of the unfrosted Bundt cake, I saw a Dresden Plate and there it began. I truly love growing fresh herbs in summer and I use them in all sorts of recipes. Mint is one of my favorites. Blueberries add wonderful color and flavor.

Cake Recipe

In mixing bowl, stir together:

    1 white cake mix
    1 box instant cheesecake
        pudding mix
    pinch of salt

In a separate bowl, stir together:

    4 egg whites
    2 tablespoons light oil
    1 cup water
    1 tablespoon vanilla
        extract
    ¼ teaspoon almond
        extract
    1 cup ricotta cheese

Add to the ingredients in the mixing bowl and blend together on slow speed for 1 minute. Stop and scrape down the bowl, and beat an additional 2 minutes at medium speed. The batter will be thick. Smooth mixture into a Bundt cake pan that has been greased and floured. Bake at 350 degrees F for 50 minutes, or until toothpick comes out clean. Cool on wire rack before inverting onto cake plate.

White Chocolate Frosting

In mixing bowl with paddle attachment, cream together:

    3 ounces cream cheese,
        softened to room
        temperature
    3 tablespoons butter,
        softened to room
        temperature
    3 ounces white chocolate
    (3 squares), melted
        and cooled to room
        temperature

Beat in:

    1½ cups powdered sugar
    1 teaspoon vanilla extract

If the frosting is too thick, add milk a very little at a time to loosen. After the sugar is incorporated, beat on high speed for at least 3 minutes. The longer the mixture is allowed to beat together, the whiter in color it becomes. This will make enough frosting to entirely cover the cake. Garnish with fresh blueberries and mint leaves.

Recipe courtesy of Ellen LaVen (Reprinted with permission)

SUMMER BUNDT CAKE WITH MINT AND BLUEBERRIES,

60" x 60". Designed, made, and quilted by Jane Zillmer.

Summer Bundt Cake with Mint and Blueberries

Finished quilt size: 60" x 60"

The Dresden Plate sections are machine appliquéd rather than pieced. I hand quilted this quilt using perle cotton and a modified "big stitch."

Fusible web and other supplies: See Resources, page 78.

Wash and press all fabrics.

Read all instructions before beginning.

Materials

3½ yards – Dark brown for the background, Border B, and Border D

⅓ yard – Brown plaid for Border A

⅓ yard – Blue marble for Border C, blueberries, and center circles

8 fat quarters – Neutral shades: cream, taupe, and honey for Dresden Plate slices

Scrap – Black for the blueberry buds

Scraps – Mint green, 2 different prints for the mint leaf clusters

1 fat quarter – Dark green for the vines and stems

1 fat quarter – Medium green for the border leaves and outer mint cluster leaves

4 yards – Backing

68" x 68" – Batting

½ yard – Binding

Dresden Plate Blocks

Finished block size: 14"

Cutting Instructions

¼" seam allowance included

❀ Background blocks – 9 squares 14½" x 14½"

❀ Border A – 2 strips 2" x 42½"
   2 strips 2" x 45½"

❀ Border B – 2 strips 4" x 45½"
   2 strips 4" x 52½"

❀ Border C – 2 strips 1" x 52½"
   2 strips 1" x 53½"

❀ Border D – 2 strips 4" x 53½"
   2 strips 4" x 60½"

Appliqué Instructions for Background Blocks

Follow the general raw-edge appliqué instructions on pages 16–19 to prepare the designs.

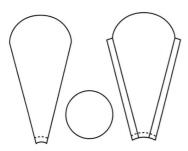

Summer Bundt Cake with Mint and Blueberries—Dresden Plate templates are full size on the CD.

❀ Prepare nine Dresden Plate motifs. For each motif you will need six of Template A and six of Template B.

❀ Using the templates, trace the motif designs onto the paper side of the fusible web. Cut out the motifs, adding an extra ¼". Cut out the inner portion of the fusible web, leaving a donut hole about ⅛" inside the traced lines. Fuse the web to the wrong side of the fabric. Cut out the shapes on the outer traced lines.

❀ Note that Template A is placed and fused over Template B. Alternating the Template A and Template B shapes, fuse 12 templates together to make a Dresden Plate motif.

❀ Mark the center point of each background block.

❀ Mark the center point of each Dresden Plate motif.

❀ Remove the paper backing, and fuse one Dresden Plate motif to each of the background blocks, matching the center points. Follow the placement diagrams below and the quilt photo on page 51.

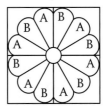

Full block diagram
for Dresden Plate Motif
Make 9

Summer Bundt Cake with Mint and Blueberries—Diagram for Dresden Plate motif. Make 9 blocks following the full block design illustration.

❀ Machine appliqué stitch in place.

❀ Join the background blocks in three rows of three blocks each.

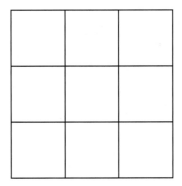

Summer Bundt Cake with Mint and Blueberries—Background block placement diagram

Appliqué Instructions for Mint Leaf Clusters

Follow general raw-edge appliqué instructions on pages 16–19 to prepare the designs.

Mint Leaf Cluster diagram

SUMMER BUNDT CAKE WITH MINT AND BLUEBERRIES— Mint Leaf Cluster templates are full size on the CD. Mint Leaf Cluster diagram: make 6 clusters.

❋ Prepare six mint leaf clusters. Set two aside for the borders.

❋ Position four mint leaf clusters over the intersections of the center blocks and fuse to the quilt top.

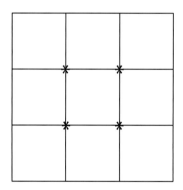

Place a Mint Leaf Cluster at each ✱.

SUMMER BUNDT CAKE WITH MINT AND BLUEBERRIES— Diagram for positioning the Mint Leaf Clusters

❋ Machine appliqué stitch in place.

Borders

❋ Sew each of the four borders to the quilt top, as shown in the diagram.

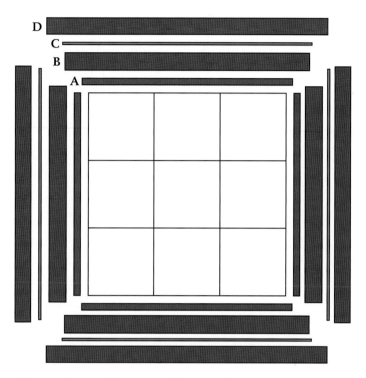

SUMMER BUNDT CAKE WITH MINT AND BLUEBERRIES— Border piecing diagram

Appliqué Borders

Follow general raw-edge appliqué instructions on pages 16–19 to prepare the designs.

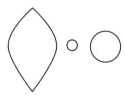

SUMMER BUNDT CAKE WITH MINT AND BLUEBERRIES— Blueberry, Blueberry Bud, and Border Leaf templates are full size on the CD.

SUMMER BUNDT CAKE WITH MINT AND BLUEBERRIES—
Vine and Stem templates and placement diagram
are full size on the CD.

❀ You will need two vines and stems and
two reverse vines and stems in addition
to the blueberries, buds, and leaves, as
indicated on the templates.

❀ It is very helpful to trace the vine diagram
onto tracing paper or an overlay material.
Lay this traced diagram on the quilt and
position the vines, leaves, berries, buds,
and leaves underneath it.

1 Lay the quilt top flat and fuse a mint leaf
cluster to the upper right corner, using the
placement diagram for exact positioning.

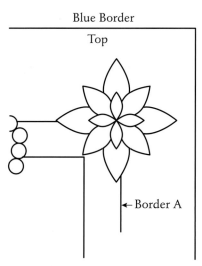

Blue Border

Top

← Border A

SUMMER BUNDT CAKE WITH MINT AND BLUEBERRIES—
Mint Leaf Cluster placement diagram for upper
right corner is full size on the CD.

2 On the vine placement diagram, note
that "TOP," the mint cluster leaf, and the
Border A markings are all landmarks for
positioning the vine starting at the top
right corner of the quilt.

3 Position a reverse vine and stem down the
right side, then position the leaves and
berries along the vine. Fuse into place.

4 Turn the diagram over to the wrong side,
and lay it horizontally across the top right
of the quilt. Using diagram landmarks for
positioning, place the vine, stem, leaves,
and berries across the upper-right top
border. Fuse into place.

❀ Rotate the quilt 180 degrees and repeat
Steps 1 to 4.

Finishing

Also see pages 75–76.

❀ Cut and piece the backing fabric to measure 68" x 68".

❀ Layer the quilt top, batting, and backing;
baste.

❀ Quilt as desired.

❀ Stitch the binding in place, and add a label
and a sleeve for hanging.

PLAIN JANE

I n 2011, I challenged my appliqué group to design and create a quilt which would represent each member's unique self in some way. We were not allowed to discuss our quilts with each other while we worked on them. At the unveiling of our finished pieces, each of us told the story of our quilt. The quilts were stunning and the stories very personal and interesting. This quilt is my "Essence of Self," as the challenge was called.

I try to find beauty in nature and the simple things in life. This is represented by PLAIN JANE's monochromatic color theme and simple flowers and branch appliqués. I let my quilts tell the story of who I am and what I see.

I machine quilted PLAIN JANE on my home BERNINA sewing machine. I used Diane Gaudynski's "Headbands" design to free motion quilt the background. This design is found in *Quilt Savvy: Gaudynski's Machine Quilting Guidebook*, written by Diane Gaudynski, AQS, ©2006.

....

56   Nature's JOURNEY Appliqué ❖ *Jane Zillmer*

PLAIN JANE, 28" x 28". Designed, made, and quilted by Jane Zillmer.

PLAIN JANE

Finished quilt size: 28" x 28"

Materials

¾ yard – Background

1 fat eighth of each – Off-white, beige, light
   brown, and pale green for appliqués

Scraps – Dark brown and gold for appliqués

1 fat quarter – Piping fabric (optional)

4 yards – Piping cording, 1mm (optional)

⅞ yard – Borders

1 yard – Backing

32" x 32" – Batting

⅓ yard – Binding

Fusible Web and other supplies: See
   Resources, page 78.

Groovin' Piping Trimming Tool™, see
   resources, page 78, (optional)

Piping or zipper foot (optional)

Wash and press all fabrics.

Read all instructions before beginning.

Cutting Instructions

¼" seam allowance included

Finished block: 23"

Background – 1 square 23½" x 23½"

Piping (optional) – 1¼" bias strips, pieced to
   the length needed.

Border A – 2 strips 3" x 23½" cut on
   the lengthwise grain

Border B – 2 strips 3" x 28½" cut on
   the lengthwise grain

Appliqué Instructions

*Follow the general raw-edge appliqué instructions
on pages 17–19 to prepare all the appliqué designs.*

Flower A
diagram

PLAIN JANE—Flower A template is full size on the
CD.

PLAIN JANE—Flower B template is full size on the CD.

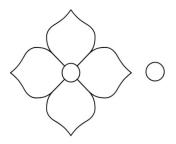

PLAIN JANE—Flower C template is full size on the CD.

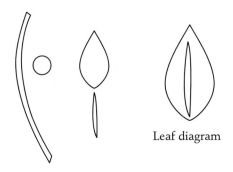

Leaf diagram

PLAIN JANE—Stem and Leaf templates are full size on the CD.

* Position the motifs on the background. Refer to the placement diagram and quilt photo for placement. I recommend pinning the motifs in place and when you are happy with the layout, fuse them to the background.

* Appliqué stitch in place.

* If using the optional piping, prepare and insert it. I recommend Susan Cleveland's Groovin' Piping Trimming Tool ™ which comes with complete instructions on how to prepare and insert piping. Also, her website (see Resources on page 78) has an excellent instructional video. Remember, the borders will be added after the piping has been sewn in place.

Borders

* Pin and sew one border A to each side of the quilt. Press the seams.

* Pin and sew one border B to top of the quilt and one border B to bottom of the quilt. Press the seams.

PLAIN JANE—Appliqué placement diagram

Finishing

Also see pages 75–76.

❀ Cut the backing fabric square 32" x 32".

❀ Layer the quilt top, batting, and backing; baste.

❀ Quilt as desired.

❀ Stitch the binding in place, and add a label and a sleeve for hanging.

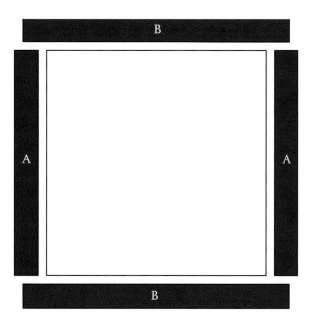

PLAIN JANE—Border placement diagram

CAMELLIA

I n March of 2010, my husband and I chose Ocean Springs, Mississippi, for our spring vacation. Winters in Northern Wisconsin are long and the Gulf Coast area is where we usually go to find warm weather. I love exploring nature when I'm traveling.

The Gulf Coast weather that year was downright cold and dreary and everything was winter brown instead of spring green. Ocean Springs residents said they had experienced the worst winter they could remember. Many perennials were lost in the cold temperatures.

The camellias, however, were in full bloom. I had never seen them before and they were beautiful in white, pinks, and reds. I knew I would have to make a camellia quilt when I got home. This photo of camellias picked outside our rental home was my starting point.

CAMELLIA, 22" x 22". Designed, made, and quilted by Jane Zillmer.

CAMELLIA

Finished quilt size: 22" x 22"

Materials

⅝ yard – Light background for inner circle

1 yard – Print for outer border

½ yard – Black for inner narrow border and binding

Appliqué Fabrics

A number of coordinating scraps – Template #11 for inner scrappy circle

Scrap – Template #12 for accent circles

1 fat quarter – Dark rose for Templates #6 and #8 for outer flower petals

1 fat quarter – Light rose for Templates #5 and #7 for inner flower petals

1 fat quarter – Light green for Templates #1 and #10 for double leaf and inner leaf

1 fat quarter – Medium green for Template #2 for middle leaf

1 fat quarter – Dark green for Templates #3, #4 and #9 for centers and outer leaf

1 yard – Backing

28" x 28" – Batting

⅓ yard – Binding

Fusible Web and other supplies: See Resources, page 78.

Wash and press all fabrics.

Read all instructions before beginning.

Cutting Instructions

¼" seam allowance included

❀ Light background – 20" x 20" square

❀ Outer border print – 28" x 28" square— oversized to allow for basting and quilting

Background and Borders

Using the 20" x 20" background square, fold it in half vertically, right sides together, and press. Then fold it in half horizontally and press. Do not unfold. See diagram 1.

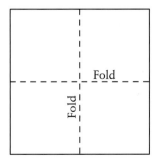

CAMELLIA—Diagram 1: Folding the background

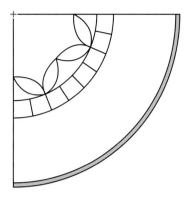

Template A for background piece is full size on the CD.

* Place Template A on the folded background piece, matching center to center. Cut the background piece on the curved line. **Don't unfold yet.** See Diagram 2.

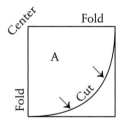

CAMELLIA—Diagram 2: Cutting the background

* Using the 28" x 28" border square, fold and press as you did the background square. See diagram 3.

* Unfold the border fabric; lay it flat with the right side up. Lay the background fabric (still folded) on the border fabric matching centers. See Diagram 3.

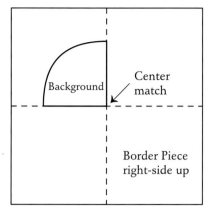

CAMELLIA—Diagram 3: Match the centers of the background and border pieces together.

* Unfold the background fabric, matching the pressed lines to the border fabric pressed lines. Both pieces are right-side up now and the circle background will be exactly in the center of the border fabric. Pin the background circle to the border fabric. See Diagram 4.

* Fold under and press a ¼" seam allowance on the background (circle) edges and pin. Stitch all around very close to the folded edge. This edge will later be covered by the inner-border strip. See Diagram 4.

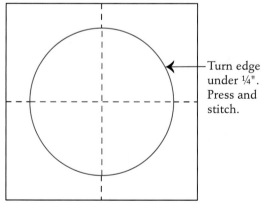

Background circle positioned on border

CAMELLIA—Diagram 4: Layering the background and border together

❊ Turn the piece over and carefully trim away the border fabric inside the stitched circle, eliminating extra bulk, and leaving a ¼" seam allowance. See Diagram 5.

❊ On the right side of the finished piece, designate and mark a "TOP."

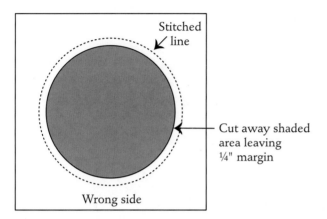

Camellia—Diagram 5: Trim the border fabric.

Now, the fun begins! You have a blank "canvas" to appliqué and your border is already in place!

Appliqué Instructions

Follow general raw-edge appliqué instructions on pages 16–19 to prepare the designs.

Be sure to mark "top" on the paper back of the appliqué where indicated on the template.

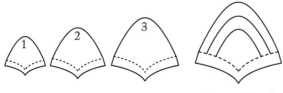

Camellia—Templates 1, 2, and 3 are full size on the CD. Layered leaf diagram: make 18.

❊ Make 18 layered leaves using templates #1, #2, and #3. Set aside 12 of these for the border.

Camellia—Center Motif diagram is full size on the CD.

❊ Place six layered leaves on a Teflon sheet. Use the center motif diagram for placement.

Camellia—Templates 4, 5, and 6 are full size on the CD.

❊ Make the center motif using templates #4, #5 and #6.

❀ Position the center motif over the six layered leaves and fuse to make one unit. Use the center motif diagram for placement.

❀ Cut out eight double leaves using Template 10. If using circles, cut out 22 using Template 12. Set aside.

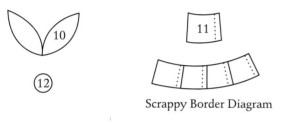

Scrappy Border Diagram

CAMELLIA—Templates 10–12 are full size on the CD. Diagram for Scrappy Border: make 8 units.

❀ For the inner scrappy circle, cut out 32 of Template #11. Be sure to mark the top of Template #11 on the paper back of each piece. Fuse together four at a time on a Teflon sheet, referring to the diagram for the scrappy border. Fuse these units to the background, overlapping each over the next to form a circle. Set aside.

❀ Make 12 outer flower motifs using templates #7, #8, and #9. Position and fuse 12 layered leaves behind six of these flowers motifs.

❀ On the background, mark circles indicated on template A for placement of the scrappy border.

Outer Flower Diagram

CAMELLIA—Templates 7– 9 are full size on the CD. Diagram for Outer Flower Motifs: make 12.

❀ Starting at the background center, pin all appliqué motifs on the background. Note all of the "top" markings, using the diagrams and quilt photo as your guide. Position all of the motifs one section at a time and **make sure all pieces fit correctly before fusing to the background.** Use the marked circle from Template A to position the scrappy border circle. The outer flowers are positioned right up to the edge of the background. The narrow black border will be stitched over that edge.

❀ Machine appliqué all motifs.

Note
   Stitch the detail lines in the flower motifs using the appliqué stitch or you can add this detail stitching when quilting the quilt.

❀ Make the narrow black border. Template A has the "Outer Narrow Border" indicated with a shaded area. Use this as your template and cut four of these pieces adding a ¼" overlap to one end of each. Join these sections together simply by turning under the ¼" overlap as you position the sections to form the circle border. Fuse into place just over the edge of the background circle, covering the edges of the border flowers. Appliqué stitch in place.

CAMELLIA—Full quilt diagram

Finishing

Also see pages 75–76.

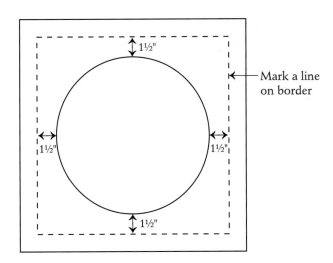

CAMELLIA – Border line diagram

❀ On the quilt top, lay a ruler at the 1½" mark at each side center. Mark this straight line, referring to the border line diagram.

❀ Layer the quilt top, batting, and backing. Baste.

❀ Quilt as desired.

❀ Quilt the border to the marked line.

❀ Straighten and square this line, if needed.

❀ Attach the binding. The marked line will be your stitching line.

❀ Trim the excess top, batting, and backing to ¼" once the binding is stitched.

❀ Turn the binding to the wrong side and hand stitch into place.

❀ Add a label and a sleeve for hanging.

Show Me a Summer Day in Missouri

My annual visits to my sister's home in southern Missouri take place in the spring when we attend the AQS quilt show in Paducah, Kentucky; how lucky am I? But I also spent a week there in August one year and found their home on a small lake surrounded by lush green flora. I collected leaves with great names and unusual shapes from trees I was not familiar with: pin oak, sweet gum, and more. I dried and pressed these leaves and used them as actual template patterns to create this quilt. It's still one of my favorite quilts, filled with not only those leaves but also wonderful memories.

SHOW ME A SUMMER DAY IN MISSOURI, 89" x 89".
Made by the author, this award-winning quilt was machine quilted by
Cheri Trexler of Arbor Vitae, Wisconsin.

. . . .

Jane Zillmer ❀ Nature's JOURNEY Appliqué   69

Show Me a Summer Day
In Missouri

Finished quilt size: 89" x 89"

Materials
Fabric

Backgrounds: Tiers A through E

    1 fat quarter – A – Very light

    ⅔ yard – B – Light

    1½ yards – C – Medium

    2¾ yards – D – Light

    4¼ yards – E – Brown, includes F corner
    blocks

Pieced borders G, center, and
corner square yin-yang appliqués

    1⅛ yards – Light

    1⅓ yards – Medium

    ½ yard total – Brown, red, green

Leaf and cicada appliqués

    ¾ yard – Gold

    1 fat quarter – Rusty brown

    1 fat quarter – Dark brown

    1 fat quarter – Medium brown

    2 yards total – Medium and dark greens

    Scraps – Black

    1 fat quarter – Gray

9 yards – backing

97" x 97" – batting

¾ yard – binding

Fusible web and other supplies: See
Resources, page 78.

Wash and press all fabrics.

Read all instructions before beginning.

Cutting Instructions for Background Tiers and Corner Blocks

¼" seam allowance included

See quilt layout diagram and tier patterns
labeled A through F.

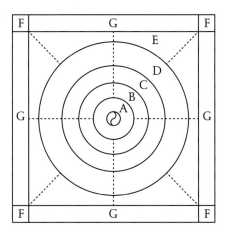

Show Me a Summer Day in Missouri—
Quilt layout diagram

The background rings are referred to as "tiers."

* Cut 1 of Tier A on folded fabric as indicated on pattern.
* Cut 4 of Tier B on fabric fold as indicated on pattern.
* Cut 4 of Tier C on fabric fold as indicated on pattern.
* Cut 4 of Tier D on fabric fold as indicated on pattern.
* Cut 8 of Tier E as indicated on pattern.
* Cut 4 of Corner F: 7¼" x 7¼" squares

Stitching Instructions for Tiers

* Piece the tier sections together as indicated on each pattern to form circles. Dotted lines on the quilt layout diagram indicate seam lines.

* Press seams open.

* Join the tiers to each other in order, A through E, matching seam lines. You will be stitching curved seams, so pin carefully before you stitch.

* Press the seams toward the outer circle.

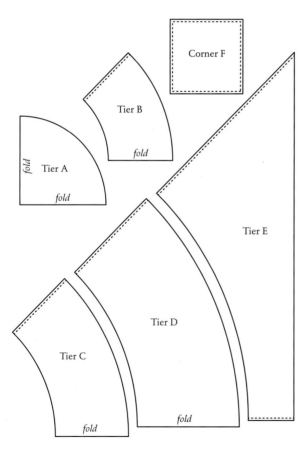

SHOW ME A SUMMER DAY IN MISSOURI—Tier templates A, B, C, D, E and Corner F templates are full size on the CD.

Appliqué Instructions for Quilt Top

Templates have not been reversed in this pattern. You will need to reverse them when tracing onto fusible web.

Follow raw-edge machine-appliqué instructions on pages 16–19 to prepare all appliqués for stitching.

See the quilt photo, page 69, for appliqué placement. It's helpful to lightly mark horizontal and vertical center lines on backgrounds by lightly pressing or using a washable fabric pencil.

Tier A

* Cut one light and one dark center yin-yang piece.

* Fuse the pieces to form a yin-yang (use the center yin-yang diagram on page 72).

❀ Place the yin-yang at the exact center of Tier A.

❀ Cut eight pin oaks and eight kousa dogwood leaves; alternate around the circle.

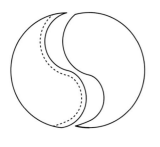 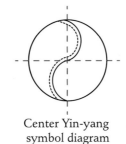

Center Yin-yang symbol diagram

SHOW ME A SUMMER DAY IN MISSOURI—Appliqué template for the Center Yin-Yang symbol is full size on the CD.

Kousa Dogwood   Pin Oak

SHOW ME A SUMMER DAY IN MISSOURI—Appliqué template for Kousa Dogwood Leaves and Pin Oak Leaves for Tier A are full size on the CD.

Tier B

❀ Cut eight sweet gum leaves and eight stems.

❀ Cut eight shingle oak leaves and eight stems.

❀ Alternate and appliqué the leaves around the circle.

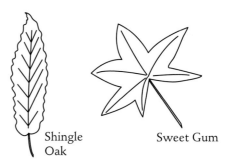

Shingle Oak   Sweet Gum

SHOW ME A SUMMER DAY IN MISSOURI—Appliqué template for Shingle Oak Leaves and Sweet Gum Leaves for Tier B are full size on the CD.

Tier C

❀ Cut eight of each sassafras leaf.

❀ Position in groups of three leaves joined with one stem.

Sassafras

SHOW ME A SUMMER DAY IN MISSOURI—Appliqué template for Sassafras Leaf Cluster for Tier C is full size on the CD.

Tier D

❀ Cut 24 hickory stems, 168 leaves, and 48 hickory nuts.

❀ Cut 24 cicada bodies and 24 cicada wings.

❀ Hickory branches are positioned around the circle, then cicadas near the outer edge.

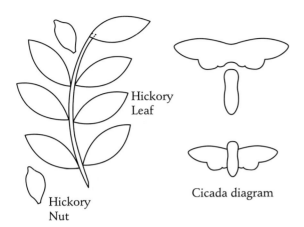

SHOW ME A SUMMER DAY IN MISSOURI—Appliqué template for Hickory Leaf, Hickory Nut, and Cicada for Tier D are full size on the CD.

Tier E

* Cut 24 red bud leaves and 24 stems.

* Red buds are placed around the circle.

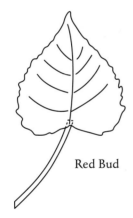

Red Bud

SHOW ME A SUMMER DAY IN MISSOURI—Appliqué template for Red Bud Leaf for Tier E is full size on the CD.

* Position the motifs on the background, pin in place. When you are happy with the arrangement, fuse the motifs. Appliqué stitch in place.

Cutting Instructions for Pieced Borders G

¼" seam allowance is included.

* Light fabric – Cut 100 squares 3½" x 3⅜".

* Medium fabric – Cut 100 rectangles 3½" x 3⅞".

* Red, brown, green – Cut 100 rectangles 3½" x 1".

Piecing Instructions for Borders G

* Make 100 units. See the Border G diagram.

* Referring to the quilt photo, piece together 25 units for each of four borders.

* Flip every other unit so that the light and medium pieces alternate.

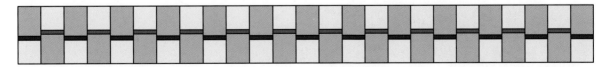

SHOW ME A SUMMER DAY IN MISSOURI—Diagram of pieced Border G

Appliqué Instructions for Corner Block F

* Follow the raw-edge machine-appliqué instructions on pages 16–19 to prepare the appliqués.

* Cut four light and four brown corner block yin-yang pieces and fuse to form yin-yangs.

* Fuse one yin-yang to each corner block F. Appliqué stitch in place.

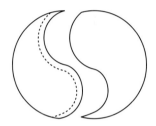

SHOW ME A SUMMER DAY IN MISSOURI—Appliqué template for Corner Block Yin-Yang is full size on the CD.

Stitching Pieced Borders and Corner Blocks to Quilt Top

* See the quilt photo for correct placement of pieced borders.

* The quilt top should measure 75½" x 75½".

* Pin and stitch one pieced Border G to each side of the quilt.

* Pin and stitch one Corner Block F to each end of the remaining two pieced Borders G.

* Pin and stitch these to the top and bottom of the quilt.

Finishing

Also see pages 75–76.

* Layer and baste the quilt top, batting, and backing.

* Quilt as desired.

* Stitch the binding in place, and add a label and a sleeve for hanging

Finishing

Binding

Once the quilt top has been quilted, it's time to apply the binding. A neat, well-constructed, and stitched binding adds a lot to your quilt. After spending all that time making a beautiful quilt, the binding should be beautiful too. I've included a few tips and my basic binding method. I really enjoy hand stitching my bindings in place!

❀ For the quilts in this book, use a double-fold, straight-grain binding.

❀ The cut binding width is a personal choice, but 2¼" is a standard width. I've used 2½" wide strips on my large quilts and 2" wide strips on my small quilts.

❀ Determine the finished quilt perimeter (the number of inches around your quilt) and add 12" for the corner turns and finishing the ends, which are cut and pieced on the bias. Add 2½" to the measurement for each seam. Divide by 40" to find the number of strips you will need to cut.

❀ Cut and bias piece the strips into one long continuous piece. Press the seams open. Using spray starch, press the long strip in half to make the double-fold binding.

❀ Use a walking foot to stitch the binding to the quilt top, batting, and backing with a ¼"

seam allowance. Miter the corners as you are stitching. Stop stitching at least 12" before you reach the starting point. Take the quilt out of the machine, finger-press a fold in each binding where they will meet, mark a center-match point on each, pin, and stitch a bias seam. Trim to ¼" and press the seam open.

❀ Trim the backing and batting to ¼". Make sure the batting and backing fills the binding when it is turned to the back.

❀ After trimming, turn the binding to the back of the quilt and hand stitch in place. Match the thread to the binding and use an invisible, close stitch. Fine tune the mitered corners as you are hand stitching to make sure the corners finish at 90 degrees.

Label

❀ Whether you show your quilts or not, always add a label to the back of the quilt. Remember that a quilt will last a long time and someone, someday, may wonder who the maker was. I've seen so many beautiful antique quilts with "Maker Unknown" included in the description. What a shame! Also, if the quilt is a gift, the recipient will appreciate that label.

❋ If you plan to enter the quilt in a contest, be sure to check the show rules regarding labels.

❋ Otherwise, simply include the quilt's name, year finished, your name, address and phone number, type of batting used, and the name of the quilter if it was someone other than yourself. If the quilt was made using a pattern, be sure to add the pattern name and designer's name. You can print the label using inkjet-printable fabric sheets or write it by hand using a permanent marker. Embellish the label as desired, maybe using the extra appliqué motifs from the quilt. Hand stitch the label to a corner of the back of the quilt. Again, check show contest rules if entering a show.

Sleeve

My last finishing touch is to add a hanging sleeve to the back of my quilts. If your quilt is never going to be hung, of course you don't need it.

❋ I always follow the American Quilter's Society instructions for hanging sleeves, printable from their website, www.Americanquilter.com. The sleeve is sewn to the back of the quilt by hand. I use an overcast stitch just at the folded edges.

Photos

I have photographed every quilt I have ever made; I keep scrapbooks and expandable files to organize and document each quilt. I really recommend this extra step.

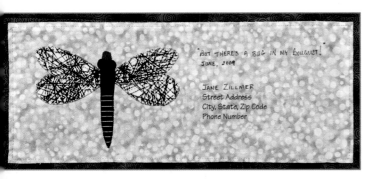

LEFT AND BELOW: Labels made by Jane Zillmer

Gallery

PINEAPPLES AND POMEGRANATES, 60" x 60", 2003. My original design. Pineapple Log Cabin blocks are bordered by Whig Rose and Pomegranate appliqués from the book *Red and Green: An Appliqué Tradition* by Jeana Kimball. Machine quilted by Common Threads Quilt Shop, Slinger, WI.

KIWI AND TARA-ITI, 40½" x 40½". Designed and made by Jane Zillmer. Longarm quilted by Lisa Arndt, Eagle River, WI. After studying images found on the www.nzbirds.com website (see Resources, page 78), with permission, I sketched some of my favorites with a folk-art flavor and chose colorful, fun fabrics to appliqué them.

BUT THERE'S A BUG IN MY BOUQUET, 89" x 89", 2009. My original design uses Electric Quilt software for layout and the traditional block pattern Friendship Bouquet. The insect appliqués are my original designs. Machine quilted by Cheri Trexler, Arbor Vitae, WI.

WHOLLY MODA!, 62" x 74", 2004. Adapted from the pattern titled FLOWERING FAVORITES from *Piece O' Cake Designs* by Becky Goldsmith & Linda Jenkins. Machine quilted by Cheri Trexler, Arbor Vitae, WI.

DRAGONFLY purse and small bag, 2010

These are my original patterns and designs. The insect appliqués were also used in I LOVE THE NIGHTLIFE.

MOON GLOW pillow, 16" x 16", 2012

This is my original design using the center motif from CAMELLIA.

Resources

American Quilter's Society:
Hanging sleeve instructions
www.americanquilter.com

BERNINA Sewing Machines
www.bernina.com

Gingher® scissors, rotary cutting mat, and tool
www.gingher.com

Schmetz sewing machine needles
www.schmetzneedles.com

Sulky® thread
www.sulky.com

Electric Quilt® design software
Inkjet Fabric Sheets
www.electricquilt.com

Compass and circle templates
www.dickblick.com

Graph paper, Sharpie® marker
Transparency film
www.staples.com

Groovin' Piping Trimming Tool™ and
Piping Cording
www.piecesbewithyou.com

HeatnBond® Lite, Pellon® Wonder-Under fusible
web, and appliqué pins—www.joann.com

Shades SoftFuse fusible web
www.shadestextiles.com

Teflon® pressing sheet
www.nancysnotions.com

Inspiration for Kiwi and Tara-Iti
www.nzbirds.com

About the Author

Jane Zillmer lives in the beautiful Northwoods of Wisconsin with her husband, Steve, and their two cats, Leo and Lily. Her sewing studio overlooks Echo Lake in Mercer. Nature and the outdoors provide many of the inspirations for Jane's appliqué designs. Retired from a rewarding career as a registered nurse, she now devotes her time to quilting, spending time with her daughters, enjoying the outdoors, and volunteering in the community.

Jane grew up in a house filled with handmade quilts. She designed and made her first quilt when she was in her teens and has also enjoyed many other needle arts over the years. In 1989, she took a beginning quiltmaking class and stitched a sampler completely by hand. She feels this was a wonderful way to learn the most basic aspects of the art of quiltmaking and she then began quilting in earnest.

After entering a local quilt show in the 1990s and winning first place, she has continued to enter local, regional, and national competitions, winning many awards.

Nine of her quilts have been juried into the American Quilter's Society contests in Paducah, Kentucky, and Nashville, Tennessee; one of them won a third-place award. Five of her quilts have been displayed at the National Quilt Association show in Columbus, Ohio; three of them received awards including: second place, honorable mention, and judge's recognition.

One of Jane's quilts was featured in the *More Quilts of Wisconsin* video by Wisconsin Public Television, and another quilt was published in the *Quilt Art 2009 Engagement Calendar* by Klaudeen Hansen, published by AQS.

Quilters Newsletter featured Jane and her quilts in the Dec/Jan 2011 issue and her quilt FLOWER POWER was published as a series quilt in *Quilters Newsletter* in 2012.

Jane shares her love of appliqué by teaching appliqué workshops and displaying her quilts whenever possible. She hopes others will develop and share her love of appliqué and quilts.

Her website: www.janezillmer.com
Her blog: www.woodsandwildflowersappliqueart. blogspot.com

Leo and Lily

more AQS books

This is only a small selection of the books available from the American Quilter's Society. AQS books are known worldwide for timely topics, clear writing, beautiful color photos, and accurate illustrations and patterns. The following books are available from your local bookseller, quilt shop, or public library.

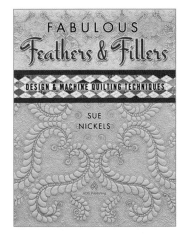

#1253

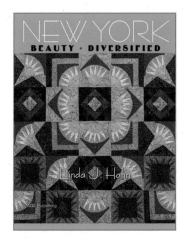

#1251

#1249

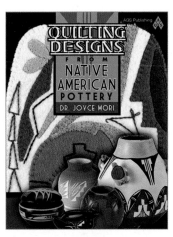

#1252

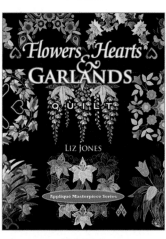

#8356

#8664

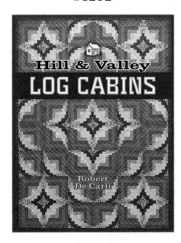

#1246

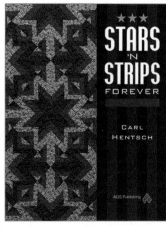

#1245

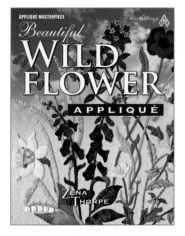

#8526

LOOK for these books nationally.
CALL or **VISIT** our website at

1-800-626-5420
www.AmericanQuilter.com